The Other Side of History: The California Native Experience

Gary Robinson
with Valentin Lopez
And Dr. Donna Schindler

© Gary Robinson 2017-2022
Published by Tribal Eye Productions
P.O. Box 1123 / Santa Ynez, CA 93460
www.LandsOfOurAncestors.com
TribalEyePro@gmail.com

ISBN: 978-1-7352003-8-5

Published by Tribal Eye Productions

"California must reckon with our dark history. California Native American people suffered violence, discrimination, and exploitation sanctioned by state government throughout its history. We can never undo the wrongs inflicted on the peoples who have lived on this land that we now call California since time immemorial, but we can work together to build bridges, tell the truth about our past, and begin to heal deep wounds."

--Governor Gavin Newsom, 2019

Contents:

1. California Historical Overview   7
2. Telling the Truth about California Missions   17
3. The Historic Road that Never Was   29
4. Hearing the Truth about Historical Trauma   39
5. Information Sources   51

PART 1:
CALIFORNIA HISTORICAL OVERVIEW

California history is commonly divided into five time periods. These are: the Indigenous period, the Spanish colonial period, the Mexican period, the gold rush, and the statehood period, which continues to the present day. Except for the Indigenous era, what happened in those periods of history has been most often told by members of the conquering, dominant societies, or the descendants of those colonial nations.

However, we're going to examine California history from more of a Native American point of view and with a slightly different objective in mind. When looking at the state's history from a California Indian viewpoint, we have to accept the very real fact that much of that history, after European contact and colonization, was traumatic and destructive for the original inhabitants of the region. That perspective is not examined or taught well or enough in our educational institutions.

So, we'll focus on these periods of California history and include the impacts these eras had (and continue to have) on California's Indigenous people.

Some of the material presented here may be new to you, but the information can be found in multiple printed sources, as well as in the oral histories of California's indigenous people, descendants of the people that experienced that history first hand. A bibliography of sources appears at the end of this book, but I've also relied on statements made by a few primary sources, including Tribal Chairman Valentin Lopez (Amah Mutsun Band of Ohlone Indians), Cross-Cultural Psychiatrist Donna Schindler, Tribal member Cherlyn Ortiz (Sierra Miwok), former Chair of American Indian Studies at UC-Davis Dr. Martha Macri (Cherokee), and Elias Castillo, author of A Cross of Thorns, which is a detailed history of the Spanish mission period.

Regarding the reliability of Native oral histories, cross-cultural psychiatrist Dr. Donna Schindler said: *For non-native people, it's incredibly difficult to hear the stories that have happened to native people in this country. For myself, every time I heard a new story, as a psychiatrist just beginning to work with Native peoples, I just didn't believe it. I read this book about Indian boarding schools, and in the book, it talked about how kids were taken away on the Navajo reservation at gunpoint, and I didn't believe it and I questioned it and I thought that couldn't be true. Who would do that? So, it took a long, long time for me as a psychiatrist, working with Native people every day, to actually get to the point where, at this point everything I hear about historical atrocities, I know it's true. I have no doubt in my mind at all, but I think for other non-native people it's a process. When you hear about the brutality of missions or the murders of Indians during the gold rush, it's very difficult, and we tend to deny things because the stories are just too much for us."*

California's Indigenous Era

The indigenous era began at least 13,000 years ago. This was an extended golden age where native people prospered with their languages, religions, and cultures intact. During this time, tribal groups from a wide range of original geographical regions, with very different languages, settled in California and the Channel Islands. Thirteen-thousand-year-old human remains found on one of the Channel Islands confirms this early date for indigenous occupation. Indigenous population estimates range from a low of 300,000 to a high of one million inhabitants before European contact. Abundant food resources from the ocean, rivers, forests, mountains and plains allowed for rich cultural diversity among indigenous groups.

Dr. Martha Macri, former Chair of American Indian Studies at UC-Davis discussed the reasons so many Indigenous groups lived here: *California, today, is a collection of people from everywhere, because it's a great place to live. Rich in resources and blessed with mild weather. That, it appears that has always been people's opinion, because the variety of tribal cultures and languages demonstrates that fact. We have many different language stocks represented and between eighty and one hundred twenty languages. There are Aztecan languages that are related to the languages of great basin and Mexico. We have the Chumashan languages in the Santa Barbara area, we have languages in the norther California that are distantly related to the Algonquin languages of the east coast and northern plains. Then we have languages, also up north, that are related to the Athabascan languages of the westerns subarctic and related to Apache and Navajo of the Southwest. So, because we can identify languages that are outside of the state that are related to some of these groups, we can infer certain kinds of movements of people into the area and linguists can hypothesize about what groups might have been in the region earlier than others.*

However, California Indigenous people are not necessarily as interested in what linguists and archaeologist think about their origin. Native American peoples, almost all the tribes, consider that they were created here. A few people have migration stories that their people came from some other region but Native people are generally not particularly interested in stories of the Bering land bridge, which is a bit outdated anyway. So, I told my students there are a lot of different ways to understand things. Based on linguistic information, we have one kind of picture; based on archeological information we have another kind of picture and based on Native tradition we have yet another kind of information. All those just need to be understood within their own context. For Native people, whose justification for existence is their connection with the land, having an eternal connection with the land is quite important and not trivial.

Spanish Colonial Period (1769 – 1821)

The Spanish Colonial Era, better known as the Mission Era, saw the first wave of immigrants arriving on indigenous lands, immigrants determined to colonize the area and use the indigenous peoples as their labor force. The missions were actually institutions of the conquest, and during that era, the Spaniards managed to deplete native populations near the missions by about *eighty percent*. In some missions, the life expectancy of a Native American laborer was two years.

Regarding this period, Tribal Chairman Valentin Lopez said: *Imagine those first Indians that were taken to the mission. The padres separate the families, they take away their culture, they take away their natural environment, they take away their spirituality, their ceremonies, their customs, their way to keep balance in their life. How do those parents teach their children to have love, to have hope, to have happiness, to know that tomorrow's going to be a better day, to know that they are good people, to know that they are important, that they have value? That did not happen.*

The Mexican Rancho Era (1821 – 1848)

The Mexican Era caused the further collapse of native populations, communities, cultures, and life ways as the missions gave way to vast ranches that also relied on forced Indian labor. One of their main products was leather goods to be shipped to the eastern US and Europe. The end of Mexican rule came after the Mexican-American War, with the defeat of Mexico in 1848.

Chairman Lopez: *During the Mexican Period, when they had these large ranches, our ancestors were forced to work on those ranches. That was another period of slavery. They could not leave. Once again, they were captured. There is a story about an Indian in 1839, I believe it was, where an Indian ran away. He wanted to get away from the ranch that he was forced to work at. The ranchers, they sent vaqueros out to capture him. They lassoed him by the neck and drug his body all the way back to the main compound and left the body hanging there for a number of days to put fear and intimidation into the Indians who were there, letting them know that if they ran away that is what would happen to them.*

The Gold Rush (1848 – 1855)

The discovery of gold in northern California in 1848 opened the flood gates of Anglo-American intrusion into the area. About 300,000 people came to the regions to seek gold. Entire native communities were enslaved or slaughtered by gold-hungry settlers who considered Indians as inconvenient obstacles to untold wealth.

Cherlyn Ortiz of the Sierra Miwok Tribe: *My tribe, which is the Sierra Miwok, was once the biggest tribe of Miwok, but during the gold rush, that's when we were almost all wiped out by diseases and by settlers, colonists, ranchers, gold miners. I think that it was a concept that everybody that came over here during the gold rush thought it was their duty to annihilate the Native Americans, so Natives suffered greatly during that period. I can only imagine the suffering and the pain that they went through. They used to get the babies and take their feet and hit them against rocks to save bullets and crush the skulls. They would kick in the back of the head with their boots to save ammunition. They would drown them as well.*

Early Statehood/American Period (1850 – 1870)

California became a state in 1850 and an American Indian killing campaign, complete with state funding, was immediately authorized by the governor and state legislature. The extermination of American Indians almost became a civic duty.

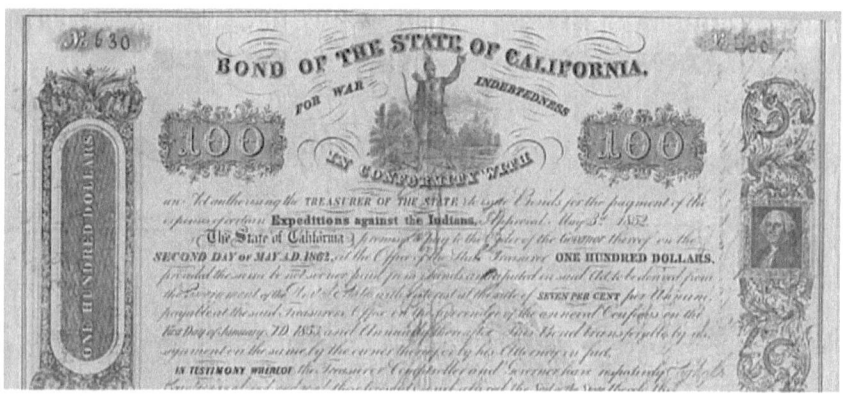

State bond to raise funds to exterminate Native Americans

The indigenous peoples of California who survived this history did so by hiding and/or disguising their true identities. Acknowledging your Native American heritage was suicide. Better to pretend to be anything but Indian. And to ensure their children's continued survival, parents often hid American Indian heritage from them.

Valentin Lopez: *The American period was incredibly brutal, incredibly horrendous to California Indians. That was the state solution to the Indian problem was extermination. The first governor, in his very first State of the Union of California, stated that there will be a "war of extermination" against the California Indians. In his words, war was inevitable. Shortly after that, a number of things happened. The state passed a treasury bond for the extermination of Indians. Can you imagine? Today we issue treasury bonds to develop schools, to develop highways, to develop waterways and et cetera. But they passed a bond here in California for the extermination of California Indians. California citizens and mostly institutions were buying treasury bonds to make profits off of the extermination of Indians. That effort there raised over $700,000. Much of that money was used to pay bounties for Indians. From twenty-five cent to five-dollar bounties were pretty normal for a dead Indian. Some people would bring in over a hundred scalps at a time and turn those in to collect their bounty. The state also paid militias to go up to the mountains to find the Indians and to kill them. In total, 1.7 to 1.8 million dollars was spent to exterminate California Indians.*

PART 2:
TELLING THE TRUTH ABOUT CALIFORNIA MISSIONS

On September 23, 2015, a Franciscan missionary named Junipero Serra was canonized or sainted by Pope Francis in spite of the angry protests by Native Americans all across the United States. Serra, founder of the first nine Spanish missions in California, has been dead for more than 230 years. But in recent times, he became a lightning rod for Native peoples fed up with the glorification of historical European explores, exploiters, colonizers and settlers. For them, Serra was, and still is, a symbol of the centuries of slavery, genocide and deculturation brought to indigenous peoples by European Christians in their quest for lands, resources and worldwide domination.

If you've ever driven down California's Highway 101, you may have noticed the historical Bell Markers that appear every mile or two along the way. Attached to some of those markers are signs that say "Historic El Camino Real." There are about 600 of those bells, maintained by the California Department of Transportation, known as Caltrans, which is funded by California taxpayers. What most people, apparently including the staff of Caltrans, don't know is that California's Camino Real was a **hoax**, part of an elaborate **myth** created by land developers, tourism boosters and imaginative writers to bring people and their money to the young state. Beginning around 1880, this myth glorified the missions and the padres while denigrating and demonizing native peoples. That myth was eventually accepted as historical fact, touted in magazines, books and films, inserted into public schools and taught to generations of California students.

The Well-Publicized Historical Myth

The Mission Myth evolved over a period of time and came to consist of four main parts. **Number 1:** California Indians were part of the most worthless race of people on the face of the earth who had to be saved and civilized at any cost. They had no culture, religion, values or real language of their own. **Number 2:** Under the heroic leadership of Father Serra, the courageous and selfless Spanish Franciscan friars successfully converted and civilized the lazy, dishonest Indians of California, who became willing and happy workers within the mission system. **Number 3**: The 21 missions were built in sequence from south to north beginning in San Diego and ending in Sonoma. They were constructed a single day's journey apart in order to provide a comfortable way-station for any non-Indian traveler that might pass that way. They were connected by a road built under Serra's supervision, called El Camino Real or the Royal Road. **Number 4:** California mission Indians loved the priests who treated the Natives only with kindness. Any discomfort or loss of Native life was due to the inferior qualities of the Indians themselves. Only serious "law-breakers" were ever punished.

Who created this elaborate historical myth and why? A generation of seemingly well-meaning people in the late 1800s and early 1900s who were more interested in building a fantasy land for future generations of Americans than they were in recording and recounting an accurate picture of history. Imaginative magazine, newspaper, book and play writers, land and real estate developers, members of elite societies and ladies clubs, educators, evangelists and entrepreneurs. They built the myth magazine story-by-magazine story, advertisement-by-advertisement, tourist-by-tourist, textbook-by-textbook, and by gullible new state resident-by-gullible new state resident.

The Truth About Serra, the Padres and the Missions

Valentin Lopez: *When Junipero Serra came to California, he was not following in the footsteps of Jesus Christ. A lot of people think that when he came here, he was an evangelizer, and he was following the footsteps of Jesus Christ. That's the furthest thing from the truth. Whenever Jesus Christ evangelized, he did not take soldiers with him.*

Fact: California mission founder Father Serra had previously been an officer of the Spanish Inquisition and believed in physical punishment for those who did not adhere to the church doctrines and practices. He also believed and practiced physical punishments for impure thoughts or acts. Self-flagellation and self-inflicted pain were part of his own personal routine. These attitudes were evident in his prescription for converting and civilizing indigenous peoples.

Elias Castillo, author of <u>A Cross of Thorns</u>, said this about Serra: *He was an agent of the Inquisition when he was in Mexico. So, he thought, obviously that the Inquisition was worthwhile and was doing its job. That was in the back of his mind. And you combine that with his fanaticism in everything he tried to do – beating himself, wearing what they called this iron mail across his chest and stomach. And it had spikes that were about half an inch long. He would cinch that up tightly. And then he would have another one that was cinched around his thigh, cinched up very tightly so the barbs would penetrate. He also used to burn himself with a torch. He would take the torch while he was preaching sermons during his time in Mexico City, and then hold the burning torch against chest, and pull it off along with the charred skin.*

In one letter, Father Serra wrote: *That spiritual fathers should punish their sons, the Indians, with blows appears to be as old as the conquest of the Americas... Two or three whippings applied to them may serve, for them and for the rest, as a warning of spiritual benefit for them all.*

Father Matthew Elshoff, a recent padre at Mission Santa Ines, explained this detail regarding the selection of missionaries: *The Franciscans didn't send their best priests to the Americas as missionaries. They sent problem priests to faraway outposts so they couldn't do damage in their home communities.*

When thinking about the twenty-one missions established by Spain in Alta California, you have to realize they weren't anything like Christian missions you think of today. Actually, the Spanish missions were intended to do much more than merely "Christianize" the Indians. They were in fact outposts of the Spanish colonial empire, and the Indians merely the labor force needed to build and maintain those outposts.

Mark Day, former Franciscan Priest said: *It would be a good idea to imagine if we had a time machine. So, we go to the mission like the one here in Santa Barbara today. Everything is climate-controlled. The gardens are beautiful. The statues are beautiful. The museums emphasize the religious aspect of the missions. But we don't see anything about the reality of what happened. If we could get into a time machine and that would bring us back, we would see something very sad.*

A Day in the Life of a Mission Indian

When Indigenous people entered the mission community they were first asked to repeat a statement that declared their belief in a strange religious system made in a foreign language they didn't understand. Once that formality was out of the way, the padres baptized the "neophytes," as they were called, gave them Spanish Catholic names and entered them in the baptismal book.

Depending on their age and gender, neophytes were divided into three groups: 1) Married couples with children under age ten. 2) Unmarried females ten years old and up, and 3) Unmarried males ten years old and up. Each group slept in separate, well-supervised quarters.

Of course, there were rules to be followed in this new religious life. You had to learn to understand and speak a foreign language. No "heathen" languages or religious activities were allowed. You had to hear the words of the black book every day, even if you didn't understand what was being read. Most importantly, you must not interact with the unmarried members of the opposite sex, and you must follow the daily schedule and perform your work duties as assigned.

Daily life within a California mission was ruled by the bells. First morning bell signaled time for morning prayers while kneeling. The second bell signaled time for breakfast, made up of food you've never seen, food that will make you sick to your stomach. You must learn to like it for that is all there is to eat. The third bell signaled time for work. Men and boys, ten and up, made adobe bricks or plowed the fields or did a dozen other manual labor jobs.

Women and girls ten, and older, scrubbed floors, made clothes, prepared food or did a dozen other manual labor jobs. The next bell signaled time for another gut-wrenching meal. Another bell, time for another gut-wrenching meal. Finally, time came for an afternoon rest. And another bell signaled time for reading from the black book, even though you can't understand what's being said. Final bell, time for your separate beds. Ding-dong, ding-dong, day in, day out.

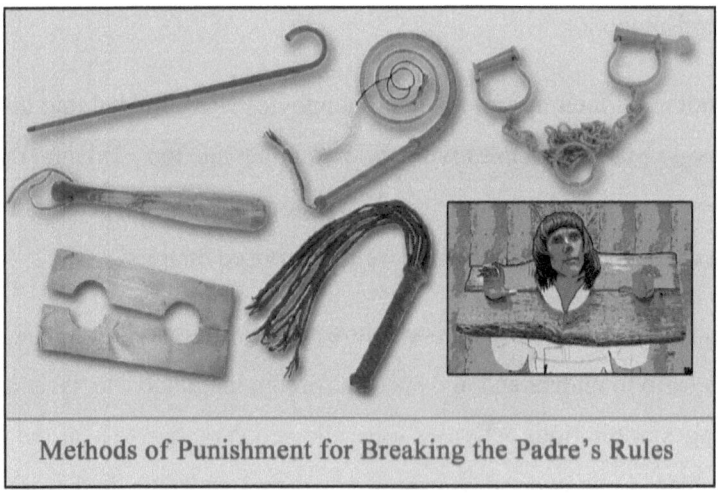

Methods of Punishment for Breaking the Padre's Rules

Any neophyte who didn't understand what was being said, who broke the padres' rules, or didn't properly do their jobs would be disciplined.

The Tools of Discipline

Here's an introduction to what mission soldiers and padres called the "tools of discipline." For the smallest infractions, like not paying attention during worship or bible readings, there's the cane. With this, the padre can reach across other worshippers to whack a neophyte across the back or head. Then there is the cudgel for quick corrections in any situation. For anyone who runs away, there are several means of preventing any further attempts, such as the leg irons and various forms of hobbles and shackles. For any unmarried woman who misbehaves with a man, the ankle stocks take care of that temptation. The great thing about shackles and hobbles is that they still allow the wearer to get his or her work done.

The whip is another instrument of correction, which creates that painful spark towards repentance. But for those who tend to break the rules over and over again, there's the Cat-O-Nine Tails. In extreme cases, each of the nine-whips could be equipped with barbs that leave a long-lasting impression.

In a letter to the commander California's Spanish colonial soldiers, Father Serra wrote: *If your lordship does not have shackles, with your permission, they may be sent from here. I think that punishment should last one month.*

The King of Spain ordered that neophytes (newly baptized Indians) could only be "trained in the ways of civilization" and religion for ten years, and then they must be allowed to return to your home communities. But in Serra's mind, the King didn't understand what "these Indians" were really like, so he decreed that Native American laborers would stay at the missions for the rest of their life to work without pay. And when they died from filth, disease, malnutrition or physical abuse, soldiers were simply sent out to round up more Native souls who needed saving.

Former Franciscan Mark Day: *The problem with the Franciscans of that period is that they were part of the apparatus of the conquest, so it was the cross and the crown. Don't forget the key word was "domination." The friars and the soldiers dominated the Indians. They destroyed their religion; they destroyed their relationship to the land; they destroyed their culture—everything was destroyed.*

Author Elias Castillo: *I found the writings of Mariano Payeras, the last Spanish president of the California missions. One of his letters I call the "smoking gun," because it's so important to understanding this history. Payeras was very frank, did not hold anything back. In his letter he said all we have done for the Indians is to baptize them, administer the sacraments, and bury them. He says we have wiped out the Indians. That's a paraphrase, but that's essentially what he said. And then, again paraphrasing, in this letter to his superior in Mexico City, he also wrote that we have to come up with an alibi that will defend us because if not, we're going to get blamed for the disappearance of the Natives and we're going to subjected to scandal and scorn.*

Chairman Val Lopez: *That is when the big lie of California's Indian history started. So, the story they created to explain what happened in California is that the Indians came to the missions voluntarily; that they came to find a better life; that they came to learn agriculture; that they came to find God. And many other such reasons as that, of why they came, why Indians went to the missions. And when you look at the missions today, the history of the California Indians is not told there.*

It doesn't say that 19,421 Indians died at Mission San Juan Batiste. When you go to Santa Cruz, it says nothing that the life expectancy for the Indigenous people there was less than two years. Today, the missions want to glorify the architecture and emphasize how holy they are. When I go to the California missions all I feel is death. I very seldom go to missions, because all I feel there is death.

Native American Burials at the Missions

One indication of how much a society values its members is how people are memorialized in death. The very clear division between the value of priests when compared to the value placed on the lives of Indians is visible in most mission cemeteries. The burial places of priests and church leaders were marked with notable symbols, crosses and memorials. On the other hand, the deaths of the Indians who built the missions, and for whom those institutions were supposedly established, were marked with nothing. The final resting place for two thousand to four thousand Indians at each mission was a mass, unmarked grave. It is estimated that more than 60,000 California Indians lie buried in mass unmarked graves in or near California missions.

Dr. Donna Schindler: *The fact that Indian people were dumped into unmarked graves at the missions tells me that they were a commodity. They were like a piece of machinery. They were worthless, didn't have a soul. They had no purpose other than to do their jobs and that was it. They weren't respected. They weren't seen as being human beings.*

What's the Moral of this Story?

What is one to take away from all this? First, we must acknowledge our true history. Even school children in Germany learn of the horrors of the Holocaust so something like that could never happen again. Second, we need to realize that California's historic missions were more like concentration camps or slave plantations than they're like Christian missions you think of today. No one is blaming the mission staff or people of the church today for what went on in the past. And finally, if you visit one of the missions, remember what kind of institution it was originally. Challenge teachers, history books, educational films and mission tour guides when they repeat the hoax and espouse the myth.

PART 3:

THE HISTORIC ROAD THAT NEVER WAS*

There is a movement afoot in California to make the historic "El Camino Real" a UNESCO "Cultural Corridor," which would place this ancient road in with a class of truly significant locations around the world. The only problem is that during the Spanish Mission era, the historical era in which this thoroughfare was supposedly created, *nothing resembling a road connecting the missions existed*. It's part of an elaborate myth that immerged in the late 1800s and early 1900s as a means of promoting the state of California as a tourism destination and economic center.

Here's how the myth goes, and remember, this is still accepted by many Californians as historical fact.

When Fr. Junipero Serra began building his "string of missions" up the California coastline in the late 1700s, he placed them about a day's journey, roughly 30 miles, apart. He needed a wagon road to connect them, so he constructed California's first highway. He called this road El Camino Real, which translates to "King's Highway" or "the Royal Road." For nearly two centuries this road, later restored and called U.S. Highway 101, was the principal north-south route in California.

That's part of the false historical view of California's "historic" missions. The truth is there was no such road during the mission era (1769-1833) or in the decades that followed. Nor were the missions built in sequence from south to north, nor were they located a single day's walk or horseback ride apart. Geographical and historical facts easily disprove parts of this myth, along with narratives written by travelers in the region during that era or shortly afterwards.

"There are many myths generated for the purpose of denying the history of genocide," wrote Nicole Lim (Pomo), Executive Director of

The California Indian Museum and Cultural Center. "The myth of El Camino Real is an example of how the colonization of California is often celebrated, portraying the decimation of native populations as necessary for 'progress' and 'civilization.'"

To begin debunking the myth, we'll start with the actual sequence in which the missions were created over a 54-year period. The process began, of course, in San Diego in 1769. The second mission was established 450 miles north on the south end of Monterey Bay in what is now called Carmel. Serra took a boat from San Diego to that location and didn't travel over land.

The third mission was San Antonio de Padua, established 1771, and located in Jolon, 80 miles south of Carmel. The fourth was San Gabriel Mission, established the same year, and located some 250 miles south of the mission in Jolon. And thus the pattern of construction continued.

As to the distance that separates the missions, the following examples disprove the "one day's journey" aspect of the myth. It is fifty-seven miles from San Juan Capistrano to the next nearest mission to the north, San Gabriel. It is sixty-one miles from the San Fernando Mission to San Buenaventura, the closest mission to the north. Yet, only eighteen miles separates Mission Santa Ines from its neighbor, La Pursima. But from La Purisma to San Luis Obispo de Tolosi is 55 miles. Finally, a mere twelve miles separates Santa Clara Mission from its neighbor, San Jose.

And then there are the traveler's narratives. Fifty recorded accounts of the missions were written by travelers who passed through Alta California during that era. This included sea captains, naval officers, explorers, scientists, clergy, merchants, fur traders, colonists and diplomats from more than twelve countries. Several of these writers characterized the missions as slave plantations. *Not one of these narratives mentions the existence of a royal road, or any road for that matter.*

Others from that group specifically commented on transportation issues and the difficulties they faced in traveling from one mission to the next. No doubt some set of paths connected each mission to its nearest neighbor, but these did not qualify for such terms as *roads* or *highways,* much less *royal*.

Thomas Jefferson Farnham published his Travels in the Californias after visiting most of the missions. The book included descriptions of the region and detailed maps. He noted that there were trails and roads that connected some Spanish colonial settlements to the nearby missions, and some that even connected the nearest seaport to a mission, but there was no road that connected the missions.

A famous traveler named Capt. George Vancouver described the journey from Mission Dolores (in the San Francisco area) to Mission Santa Clara that included a few unconnected trails. The route, he wrote, "was quite bad in spots, especially a 6-mile area where our horses were generally knee-deep in mud and water."

Alfred Robinson's description of the route from Mission San Antonia to Mission Soledad goes like this: "We traveled slowly, owing to our miserable horses and the almost impracticable state of the route which in many places extended across the mountains in narrow pathways, and was so obstructed with rocks, that I was obliged every few moments to dismount and walk."

A Swedish gentleman, G. M. Waseurtz of Sandels, traveling a few years later wrote that the route from Mission Santa Barbara to Mission San Bonaventura "led along the beach and at high water was not passable. A person overtaken there by the tides could drown without help or prospect of escape for the side of the coast is perpendicular and smooth."

Traveling the fifty miles from La Purisma to San Luis Obispo in the 1830s to perform his duties as clerk in the hide and tallow trade, Faxon Dean Atherton wrote in his diary "in some places there is no sign of a road or anything to guide a traveler."

Also in that diary we find Atherton's description of the stretch between Santa Barbara and Santa Ines as "almost impossible to descend, being in some places literally perpendicular. The distance from top to bottom in a straight line might be about one mile, but the only possible way of descending is by a zigzag course of about four, and as rocky and uneven as can well be imagined."

In 1850, a California resident named Edwin A. Sherman visited every mission, and he wrote that no Camino Real was marked on any map, and there was only a trail that connected a few points, but not many. Later, in 1905, he was among the most vocal opponents of spending state funds on the design and construction of any modern road so named.

James M. Guinn, founder of the Historical Society of Southern California, was thoroughly versed in the earlier writings of the narratives of Vancouver and others of the mission era, and he, too, objected to any attempt to name any state roads after the mythological El Camino Real.

What should be considered the final nail in the coffin of California's El Camino Real comes from Elias Castillo, author of <u>A Cross of Thorns:</u>

The Enslavement of California's Indians by the Spanish Mission. Castillo spent eight years researching material for the book in every archive containing documents and letters of the Spanish Mission era. Able to read 18th century Spanish documents, he easily translated letters from Junipero Serra and others of that time.

"There was no El Camino Real during that period," he said during a recent interview. "There is no proof that what is now identified as El Camino Real ever existed."

Castillo confirmed that during those eight years of research he never found a single document that mentioned the ordering of supplies, materials or tools for the construction of this road. Nor were there any mentions of Spanish or Indian laborers designated to build this road. The whole idea is conspicuous by its absence.

Some point to the 1775-76 expedition of Juan Bautista de Anza as the official establishment of this road. True, this expedition, which brought a group of Spanish settlers to Alta California, did blaze a trail to or near mission sites, but this trail never became anything more than a seldom used trail.

It should be noted that there really was a Spanish-built El Camino Real that connected Mexico City to the Spanish Colonial Capital of Santa Fe, New Mexico. It largely followed trails initially established by Indigenous people who were already traveling north to south to trade with distant Native communities.

So how and why did the rosy story of the peaceful and productive missions created by compassionate and visionary Spanish padres come into existence?

Beginning almost fifty years after the Mission Period ended, new California residents, who were mostly Anglos, were looking for a cultural and historical context for their lives. They were also looking for reasons to be proud of their state and messages that could attract tourists, businesses and new residents to move there.

From the 1880s to the 1920s, real estate developers, state boosters, tourism marketers, writers, educators, Catholic and Protestant religious promoters, women's clubs, automobile clubs, regional magazines, playwrights, and newcomers romanticized the mission era to fill that need. Each new writer, imagining a glorious and romantic bygone era, added something new to the myth, so it grew and flourished, and *people believed it.*

Soledad Mission Ruins - circa 1880

"With the colonial invasion and then the capitalist development of California and the social construct of society based on exploitation, capital accumulation, and racism, this is the background that necessitates the myth," said Marcus V. Lopez, Chairman of the Barbareño Chumash Tribal Council of Santa Barbara. "The master narrative must be challenged by those individuals and groups of indigenous nations and others. The honoring of El Camino Real is like honoring the paths of Hitler's SS as they organized its infrastructure in Nazi Germany."

A coalition of groups in the first decade of the 20th century pushed for the restoration of the so-called King's Highway. The idea for an historical highway came out of something called the "good roads movement," founded by people wealthy enough to own automobiles. Supporters included the newly formed Camino Real Association, the Auto Club of Southern California and several women's organizations. A quick examination of the logo of the Auto Club of Southern California reveals an unmistakable mission bell at its center.

Mrs. A.S.C. Forbes and an early bell marker

The idea of using mission bells as the main symbol for this supposed "restored highway" came from Mrs. A.S.C. Forbes, the woman who founded the California Bell Company, the only bell-making company in the Western U.S. at the time. The first such bell was installed in Los Angeles in 1906. A few short years later, California voters approved of the idea of creating Highway 101 as a restored El Camino Real to connect southern and northern regions of the state. By that time the King's Highway Myth had taken solid root within the population.

Today, state taxpayers are forced to support the reminders of this historic road that never was, because CalTrans maintains the 600 bells that appear every mile or two along state Highway 101, along with the periodic signage proclaiming "Historic El Camino Real."

"By lifting the veil of falsehoods, we can examine the bias, Nicole Lim added. "Regardless of religious intentions, Spanish colonizers targeted large-scale indigenous populations for conversion and servitude, resulting in high rates of mortality from violence and disease. We must reframe the context of history through the inclusion of Native American perspectives and contributions."

Looking to the future, Barbareño Chairman Lopez said, "Let's celebrate indigenous peoples by telling the truth and decolonizing these narratives, allowing us to maintain and continue our own narratives that bring about a brighter future, free of exploitation in all its forms."

Originally published in the Fall 2017 edition of
News from Native California

PART 4:
FOR NATIVE AMERICANS, CALIFORNIA HISTORY EQUALS HISTORICAL TRAUMA

According to Dr. Schindler, five hundred years of genocide and forced assimilation into dominant societies has caused a "scar" on people throughout the world, on Indigenous people in particular. It has been proven that this psychological scar can be passed down from generation to generation. It's called historical trauma, also known as intergenerational trauma, which refers to it being passed down from one generation to the next. It is a form of Post Traumatic Stress Disorder (PTSD), but some Native elders simply call it the <u>Soul Wound</u>.

It began in the mission era for Native Americans living near those institutions, when families were separated from one another and their languages, cultures and even their abilities to nurture the following generations. That impacted two or three generations during the mission times. And continuing for another one or two generations during the Mexican era. And continuing for another two, three, four, five generations during the American period where there's no hope, no love.

Regarding her own tribe's trauma, Sierra Miwok Native Cherlyn Ortiz said: *Where my grandfather is from, they have a creek up there that I used to play by. You could hear babies crying around that creek. I asked by cousins, "What is that?" And they said, "Oh, don't worry. It's just the water babies." And I asked, "What are the water babies?" She explained that a long time ago when the (U.S.) military was there, they herded all kinds of Native Americans from all tribes and all peoples. They took all the Indians, they herded them, they forcefully walked them up there to Mendocino County, a small town called Round Valley where my grandfather's from. Anyway, they would take the babies and drown them under the water, and that's where the name came from, the water babies, because the spirits are still there near the creek.*

Hearing and Believing the Truth

Professor Deborah Miranda once said: *There is nothing harder than being a California Indian in California, teaching California Indian Studies. There is so much mythology that you have to plow through and undo to get to the historical truth.*

In a recent interview, Elizabeth Fasthorse (Rincon tribe, Native American studies student) said: *I think to myself, people, they don't believe that those things happened, and here I am, a living, breathing human being who experienced a little of it in my lifetime.*

(Even though Elizabeth's experiences at a mission school weren't as severe as those of her ancestors at Mission San Luis Rey, she got a memorable taste of mission trauma during her school years.)

Elizabeth: *I attended Pala Mission School, or Mission San Antonio de Pala, and I started there in 1960 in kindergarten, and I went from kindergarten all the way through eighth grade. The school was run by the Sisters of the Blessed Sacrament. We went to school there for free, the natives in the area. It was totally populated with a lot of natives from the different reservations. One time I got slapped in the face and my nose bled, by Sister Marie Dushane. I'll never forget her name. This is a horrible, horrible, humiliating disgrace, if you will. I'll never forget that. Everything that happened to me was so humiliating that it made me feel like I was inferior. It made me feel like I didn't have a voice. It made me feel like I didn't exist. That I was unimportant.*

Recently, Elizabeth attended an educational workshop that gave participants a glimpse of a day in the life of a mission Indian. This workshop introduced the tools of discipline used by the padres on her Native ancestors. The workshop presenter punctuated the experience with the ringing of a small bell reminiscent of the mission bells that regulated all phases of Spanish mission life.

Elizabeth: *I never thought a bell could ring so loud in my memories, but it did. Because, that bell signified that we were bad, and something was going to happen and it brought back those memories of all those things: the punishments, the getting slapped on the hands, getting put in the corner, getting put in the closet, being put in the aisle of the church, being made to kneel with the nuns, being punished when I didn't go to church on Sundays. All that bell did was bring back all those memories.*

Self-identity – A Casualty of Historic Trauma

Catherine Herrera, an Ohlone Native resident of San Francisco, was raised to believe her indigenous roots were from Mexico, not California. One day, later in life, she once again pestered her father to get more details about their family heritage, a subject everyone in her family usually avoided.

Catherine: *And so, he finally blurted out, "We're California Natives." That was a huge shock for me. How silly I felt to be in Mexico and not really understanding or knowing that I had California Native roots. That was quite common among California Natives. A lot of California Native people had that experience, and that because it was dangerous to identify as Indian, a lot of people hid themselves. So that was very eye-opening for me and really the beginning of this journey for the last 17 years. I've become more involved with the Ohlone community because as I got to know my other cousins who I'd never met before, they also had been told that we were Ohlone. One cousin decided to go get a DNA test, and then another one, and so that part of the story started building up as well. But I'm called an "undocumented Ohlone." We do not have our mission records. We're not just sort of objective people when we're looking for our family records. There's so much tied up into it, and it's often difficult to go to the very church or the very mission archives where your family may have passed away and bad things happened and ask them for the proof of who you are as a Native person.*

How the Soul Wound Manifests in Peoples' Lives

Dr. Schindler: *Historical trauma unfortunately manifests itself in some pretty difficult ways in people's lives. People who suffer from historical trauma tend to have high, high rates of domestic violence, so what that has to do with is that when a person has been oppressed or victimized, they often turn around and victimize someone else. Most often they victimize someone in their own family. There is actually a psychological mechanism behind that, which is that when you've been victimized and oppressed, in order to feel better about yourself, you identify with the oppressor. Domestic violence is one of the biggest problems within native populations in the United States and indigenous people in the world.*

Domestic violence is one of the symptoms of historical trauma

Native American psychologist Dr. Eduardo Duran, who is the leading author in the field of the soul wound, compared the process of intergenerational trauma to the mythology of the vampire. Everybody knows when a vampire bites its victim, the victim becomes infected and also becomes a vampire. Similarly, the soul wound is transmitted from generation to generation.

Cherlyn Ortiz: *As Native American people, they say that we live through Post Traumatic Stress Disorder on a daily basis. We're prone to anxiety; we are prone to suicide. The mortality rate is the highest amongst Native Americans. We die of--typically, most of us die of heart disease, and it could be caused by diabetes or a number of other different things. Yes, it's affected us and it's still affecting us. It's historical trauma, it's something so deep and so horrendously severe that it's carried on through generation to generation. It's handed down inadvertently.*

Valentin Lopez: *Suicide is huge in our tribe. The year before last year we had a 58-year-old adult male commit suicide, and his son has just gotten married three weeks before, and then he committed suicide. Three weeks after that we had another member in their 50s, mid-50s, commit suicide by taking pills, and then she was rushed to the hospital, and she survived. I had to go talk to her and I said, "What happened?" And she said, "I understood why he did it. He just wanted to stop feeling the pain," she says. "And I realized that I, too, want the pain to stop and that's why I did it."*

Dr. Schindler: *Another part of historical trauma, another way it manifests is in terms of numbed-out feelings. Just as when a person goes off to war and they experience horrific things, they come back and their feelings are numbed out or shut down. When the same thing happened to people that suffered in the missions and during the gold rush, they have to shut down their feelings because it's just too intense to have these severe feelings of depression and despair. They go through life like that, and that makes it incredibly hard, for instance, to parent your children. If you can't feel yourself, then you're unable to help them in the world.*

Cherlyn Ortiz: *For California Natives, how we feel and how we suffer--it could have happened yesterday, you know? Just because it happened a long time ago doesn't mean anything. It's just as alive and it's just as rampant, just as strong as it was then. A lot of us do not know what it is exactly or how to deal with it.*

Dr. Schindler: *In general, across the United States, Native Americans who have been oppressed and abused and have had their cultures and traditions stripped from them are unable to heal their own soul wound because their spiritual practices were taken away, their language and their traditional ways of doing things, their relationship with the land was taken away and changed so dramatically. These days, people are working really hard to heal. For the last twenty or thirty years, people have been working very hard, and the Native people are understanding what the problem is for themselves. But they didn't even know what it was more than twenty or so years ago. They didn't realize that historical trauma was their big issue. Now that they're learning about this and understanding this, they can begin to heal themselves, but it's very difficult because their traditional ways of healing themselves were ruined.*

Valentin Lopez: *As a chairperson, I'm an advisor to the National Alliance on Mental Illness. I deal a lot with mental illness and a lot with addictions and things like that, and our tribal members know that. So, I get a lot of calls from my members when they want help. They're reaching out. One week I got four calls from members, because of addiction they were losing their children to adoption. Addiction to meth of a sixty-seven-year-old. Another person looking at a very long time in prison because of drugs, et cetera. I'm sitting there in one week and I say something's got to stop. We have to stop this.*

What Can Prevent or Delay Healing from the Soul Wound?

There are definitely a few things that delay the healing process for Native people in this country. In recent history, one of the biggest was canonizing Father Junipero Serra as a saint. <u>Hiding the truth</u> is the biggest problem in healing the soul wound. If the truth is not told, it is very difficult for the soul wound to heal. Schools have been hiding the truth forever and telling children that the missions were treating the Indians like children, that they were happy there and they learned all sorts of good things. The same thing happened in the gold rush. We hear all sorts of stories about the gold rush. Well, actually it was hugely destructive and detrimental to the Native people.

What Leads to the Healing of the Soul Wound?

According to Dr. Schindler, understanding the whole process of how historical trauma works opens the door, and then people can heal in a wide variety of ways. Basically, when you explain historical trauma to someone, you're really going back into that person's own history.

Dr. Schindler: *I have one family I work with, and I work with three generations at one time in the room actually doing tele-psychiatry, and we talk about how the great-grandmother acted towards the grandmother, how the grandmother has acted towards her daughter, how the daughter was a methamphetamine addict for many years and how she treated her own kids. We trace it back. Why did so-and-so do this? Why did great-grandmother act like this? Well, did she go to boarding school? And that's how we kind of work out... It's a puzzle. Why do people act the way they act?*

Valentin Lopez: *I applied for a grant that just happened to come to us, a wellness grant. We were so lucky. We got the wellness grant, and we started having wellness meetings. That was six years ago. At our wellness meetings we talk about our culture, our history, our traditions, our ancestors, our spirituality, et cetera. But we also talk about current issues. We talk about the suicides, the addictions, the violence, the incarcerations, et cetera.*

One of our meetings was dedicated to helping our youth recognize the importance of finding a good mate, and what came up there was the importance of being healthy. You cannot have a healthy relationship or healthy marriage if both sides are not healthy. I tell the members we have to get healthy and the way we get healthy is by returning to our culture, our spirituality, our prayers, recognizing our obligation and returning to the path the creator asked us to follow. That's how we get healthy.

People Need to Know that Healing is Possible

Cherlyn Ortiz: *With the proper guidance, the proper counseling from a loved one, an elder, somebody in their community, a doctor--a lot of help I received was through a wonderful doctor that I know. She came along at the right time, and my life is nothing short of transformed because of her. Anyway, you have to know how to deal with it, take the necessary steps. It can be done. It's a hard, tough process, but it can be done. You can come out on the other side with true peace in your heart and a deep appreciation for who you are, a deep gratitude to the creator that you were born a Native American.*

The Role of Native Spirituality

Native American spirituality, Native American religious traditions, can have an important role in the healing process.

Valentin Lopez: *I ask Native people, all Native people, to not give up on their indigenous spirituality. That is where the truth lies. Our people will not allow falsehoods to be told about others. Our religion will not allow the brutality, the enslavement, the cruelty to other people. Our religion is about relationships. It's how we have relationships with creator. How we have relationships with our ancestors, with our future descendants, how we have relationships with living people today. And beyond that, how we have relationships with the environment, our relationships with the water, with the wind, with the wildlife. Those are all relationships given to us by creator that must be valued.*

Finding Peace

Cherlyn Ortiz: *My heart breaks daily for my people, and I wish that there were better ways that I can serve them and help them deal with this intergenerational trauma, this historical trauma, because it is a very real thing, and it does exist. I know because I suffered from it for a great deal of my life, but now I find myself at peace. I find myself at peace, and I want the same thing for all of the Native Americans that have intergenerational trauma. There's always hope. If there's life, there's hope.*

We pray for our ancestors. We pray for our elders. We pray for healing from historical trauma. We pray for our spiritual wellness. We pray for our young generations. We pray for our fathers and mothers. We pray for strength. We pray for our Mother Earth.

Dr. Donna Schindler, who has been treating historical trauma in indigenous communities for over 25 years, had one last conclusion to add: *Due to unhealed historical trauma, we have epidemic rates of depression, poverty, suicide, substance abuse, domestic violence and even diabetes due to poor eating habits in Native communities in California and elsewhere. People self-soothe (or self-medicate) by drinking alcohol, taking drugs, and eat large quantities of bad food.*

Native people themselves often don't understand what's happening to them or why they're suffering.

Non-native people sometimes ask what they can do to help. The first thing is to acknowledge that California's history was brutal to the region's first inhabitants. Don't be among those who try to deny this history, and make sure this history is accurately taught as well as discussed openly. I've spoken to adult Californians who don't know early statehood history and refuse to believe that any Anglo Christian would ever do what those white protestants did. Secondly, whenever speaking to a Native person or interacting in some way with a Native community, just remember it's a miracle that any Native people even survived this catastrophic history. You don't need to say anything about it, but this knowledge may impact how you relate to indigenous people alive today.

A final word from Chairman Valentin Lopez provides us with guidance on how to respond to those who would perpetuate the false narrative: *What I ask of all people, Native and non-Native, is that they insist that the true history of California be told. Don't allow that history that was told in our schools, the history that was told by state parks, by bell markers, the Catholic Church—that false history—don't allow that to continue. Insist that the truth history be told.*

Teach the Truth About California History

SOURCES OF INFORMATION

Primary Sources

Dr. Donna Schindler – This cross-cultural psychiatrist has worked with indigenous people in New Zealand, Navajo Nation and California and has been addressing historical trauma issues for more than twenty-five years.

Chairman Valentin Lopez - Tribal Chairman Valentin Lopez has been working tirelessly for the benefit of his tribe and other Native Californians to correct falsehoods in history and make the church accountable for its maltreatment of Indians during the Mission Era.

Dr. Martha Macri – As the former Chair of American Indian Studies at UC-Davis, this enrolled Cherokee established the John P. Harrington database as a means of more efficiently studying California Indian languages.

Cherlyn Ortiz (Sierra Miwok) – A tribal community activist working to help other California Natives heal from historical trauma.

Elias Castillo (1939-2020) – Award-winning journalist and author who spent eight years researching and writing <u>A Cross of Thorns: The Enslavement of California's Indians by the Spanish Missions</u>. This non-fiction work is being widely used in several colleges and universities in the state for studying California history.

Dr. Deborah A. Miranda – Writer and poet; Professor of English at Washington & Lee University; Author of Bad Indians: A Tribal Memoir published by Heyday Books. Member of the Ohlone Costanoan Esselen Nation and a Chumash desendant.

Elizabeth Fasthorse – Native American Studies graduate student and member of the Rincon Tribe in Southern California. She is the former program coordinator in the Education and Cultural Learning Department for the Tataviam Band of Mission Indians.

Bibliography

1. Castillo, Elias. A Cross of Thorns: The Enslavement of California's Indians by the Spanish Missions. Craven Street Books, Fresno, 2015.

2. Fogel, Daniel. Junipero Serra, the Vatican, and Enslavement Theology. Ism press; San Francisco, 1988.

3. Costo, Rupert and Jeannette, Ed. The Missions of California: A Legacy of Genocide. The Indian Historian Press, San Francisco, 1987.

4. Robert H. Jackson and Edward Castillo. Indians, Franciscans and Spanish Colonization, UNM Press, Albuquerque, 1995.

5. Jean Francois de la Perouse. Life in a California Mission (Monterey in 1786), Santa Clara University and Heyday Books, Berkeley, CA 2007.

6. Deborah A. Miranda. Bad Indians: A Tribal Memoir. Heyday, Berkeley, CA 2013.

7. Steven W. Hackel. <u>Children of Coyote, Missionaries of Saint Francis</u>. University of North Carolina Press, 2005.

8. John P. Harrington's field notes from Maria Solares, Fernando Librado and other Native California consultants. Available through the J.P. Harrington Database Project located in the Culture Department of the Pechanga Tribe near Temecula, California.

9. Sherburne F. Cook. <u>The Conflict Between the California Indian and White Civilization</u>. University of California Press, 1976.

10. Phoebe S. Kropp. <u>California Vieja: Culture and Memory in a Modern American Place</u>. University of California Press, Berkeley and Los Angeles, 2006.

Educational Films

1. *Telling the Truth about California Missions*; Written and Produced by Gary Robinson; Tribal Eye Productions 2017.

2. *Hearing the Truth about Historical Trauma*; Written and Produced by Gary Robinson; Tribal Eye Productions 2018.

3. *The Other Side of History: The California Native Experience*; Written and Produced by Gary Robinson; Tribal Eye Productions 2019.

About the Author/Editor

Gary Robinson (Cherokee & Choctaw descent) is the author of twenty books on Native American topics, including both fiction and non-fiction works, and is the producer of more than one hundred television and video documentaries and educational films. His most recent fictional book, Billy Buckhorn and the Book of Spells, published in January, 2023, by 7th Generation/Native Voices Books.

His historical novel series Lands of our Ancestors, with available Teacher Guides, has been praised by educators and students alike. Intended for use in fourth grade, the series follows three generations of a California Indian family as they experience and struggle to survive the main eras of California history.

His recent educational film productions focus on the impacts of California history on the lives of Native Americans. These films include *Telling the Truth about California Missions*, *Hearing the Truth about Historical Trauma* and *The Other Side of History: The California Native Experience*. He has both BA and MA degrees in Television/Film Production.

www.ingramcontent.com/pod-product-compliance
Lightning Source LLC
Chambersburg PA
CBHW020549080526
44583CB00013B/1060